Polish 17pdr Achilles IICs from 2. dywizjon, 1. Pułku artylerii przeciwpancernej, 1. Dywizji Pancernej (2nd Squadron, 1st Anti-Tank Regiment, 1st Armoured Division) accounted for this Jagdpanther s.H.Pz.Jg.Abt.559 while it was retreating towards the Moerdijk Bridge in early November 1944. **PISM**

On 1 November 1944, a small convoy of vehicles from s.H.Pz.Jg.Abt.559 had been making their way to the bridge over the river Maas at Moerdijk from Raamsdonksveer. The convoy consisted of a captured Mark III scout car, two Jagdpanthers with damaged guns, two 18 ton Sd.Kfz.9s, a VW Schimmwagen and the maintenance squad. The convoy was spotted by units of the 1st Polish Armoured Division near Heikant and initially was not fired on, probably because of the captured Mark III scout car, but while driving at full speed towards Zevenbergsche Hoek the second Jagdpanther received fire and was hit. The unit history says that it was hit in the running gear, but the only visible penetration is in the hull side. The crew baled out and the other vehicles picked them up. These two photos show curious Polish soldiers looking over the wreck. Note the unit insignia on the front mudguard - unfortunately indecipherable.

2x PISM

The s.H.Pz.Jg.Abt.559 had converted to Jagdpanthers, and Sturmgeschütz III, from 7.5cm Pak 40 auf Sfl. 38(t) between May and September 1944. Immediately after receiving the last of the Jagdpanthers, the unit was immediately transferred to the front. Our vehicle has a sectional 8.8cm Pak 43/3, twin driver's periscopes with inverted 'V' shaped rain guard and Zimmerit. The graffiti on the glacis plate reads: 'II Dyon', an abbreviation of Dywizjon, meaning squadron. The 1st and 2nd squadrons were equipped with the Achilles, the 3rd and 4th with towed 17pounder guns.

3x PISM

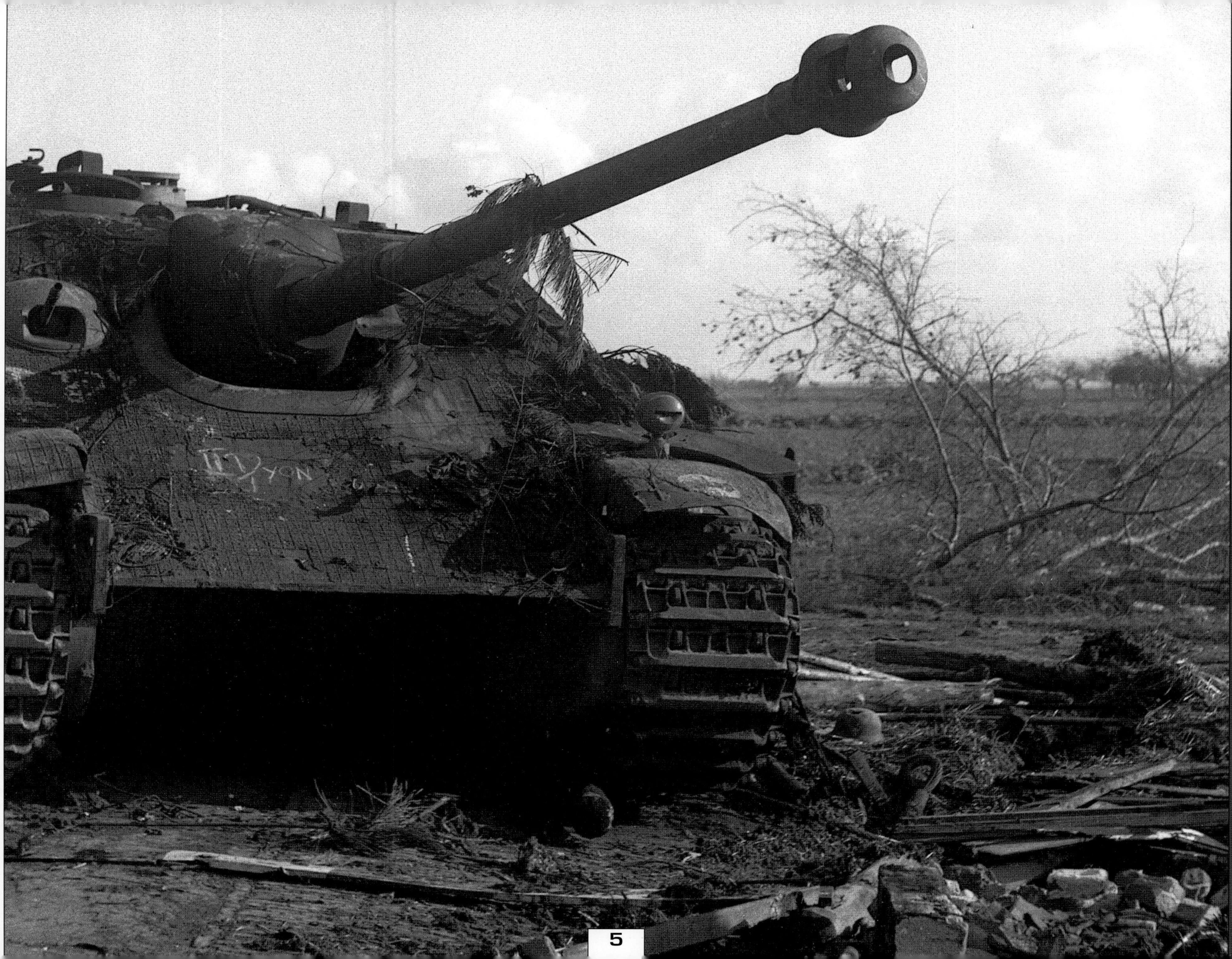

The side of the Jagdpanther showing the penetration in the side of the fighting compartment, close to the gunner's position. The impact has blown the tool rack from the hull side & started a fire that has led to the suspension sagging. The engine access door is open on the engine deck and the two square shaped air filters have been stacked on the engine deck.

PISM

The vehicle photographed much later. The tracks have been removed and it has been pushed off the road to sink into the mud. An explosion has blown open or blown away nearly all of the hatches, including the kidney shaped gunsight cover and the Nahverteidigungswaffe just behind. With the camouflage materials now gone we can see the inverted 'V' shaped rainguard over the driver's periscopes. **PISM**

These two Panther Ausf.G from I./Pz.Rgt.39, 17.Panzer-Division were knocked out either side of a railway line in the village of Bolatice, Czechoslovakia on 16 April 1945, at 10.00 to be exact. The vehicles had been silenced by two T-34/85s of 2nd Battalion, 1 CS Independent Tank Brigade commanded by Sgt. Danca and Cpl. Penkert. These tanks in turn were knocked out by two Pz.IV/70(V)s, one of which is shown on page 12. The lower photo shows the lead Panther that has a Russian recovery marking of ZB-387 on the glacis plate. The white object on the mudguard would have said that the tank was knocked out by the 1 CS Independent Tank Brigade, but unfortunately we cannot see this. **2x VHU**

The rear Panther, recovery marking ZB-386. Some interesting details can be noted here: the fitting on the turret rear side for mounting a spare wheel, the watering can hooked over the left exhaust pipe, and the interlocks of the cast turret front plate sticking out proud of the turret side. A careful look at the commander's cupola shows also that it is missing an armoured periscope cover. An abandoned German boot at the rear of the vehicle adds a human touch to the scene.   **VHU**

Front and side of the rear Panther. The front Schürzen plates have had their corners rounded and a number have come off, presumably because of the destruction of the vehicle. Both the driver's and radio operator's hatches have been jettisoned, either by the crew escaping or by an explosion. The photos on page 11 were taken after that of page 10 as the tank is missing the Bosch headlamp and the hull MG ball mount plug with chain.
3x VHU

11

Two shots of one of the Pz.IV/70(V)s of 17.Panzer-Division that knocked out Sgt. Danca's and Cpl. Penkert's T-34/85s at Bolatice. This vehicle was probably knocked out by 2nd Lt. Popovic of the 3rd Battalion, 1 CS Independent Tank Brigade. Popvic's T-34/85 was behind the house visible in the background of the lower photo and by opening a door and a window he knocked out the German vehicle by quite literally firing through the house! The resultant explosion unseated the fighting compartment and blew the roof off. The vehicle had three return rollers and Flammentöter exhausts. **2x VHU**

Pz.Jg.Abt.3 of 3.Panzergrenadier-Division lost this Pz.IV/70(V) while attempting to stop armour from the US 3rd Armoured Division at Cherain, Belgium on 16 January 1945. Two Pz.IV/70(V) of Pz.Jg.Abt.3 supported by five Panthers, probably from I./SS-Pz.Rgt.9 knocked out 4 US Shermans and effectively halted the attack, until US artillery laid down a barrage. It has lost a track and a return roller and although difficult to see, it has two resilient steel wheels on the first suspension bogie. Remnants of camouflage paints are barely discernible on the gun mount and mantlet.
2x NARA

Pages 14 - 16: Two minutes up the road from Cherain lies a Panther Ausf.G of I./SS-Pz.Rgt.9 (not Pz.Rgt.9 as widely believed) which was knocked out by a shot in the rear plate. Some sources state that it took three rounds, but the photo on page 16 just shows one. It had hit a Sherman tank - perhaps the one in the background - and was subsequently knocked out by an M-36 tank destroyer of the 703rd Tank Destroyer Battalion in a deadly game of tit for tat. The photo on page 16 shows quite graphically how the round penetrated the rear plate, blowing off the armoured exhaust. A secondary explosion most likely blew the rear hatch out of the turret.
3x NARA

Another of the I./SS-Pz.Rgt.9 Panthers knocked out during the US attempt to take Cherain, Sterpigny and Brisy on 16 January. Like many Panthers, including the one on the preceding pages, the torsion bars have sagged after a fire, giving the tank a lower than usual stance. **NARA**

As U.S. troops entered Czechoslovakia in May of 1945, General Eisenhower set the halt line at Karlovy Vary – Pilsen – České Budejovice. An agreement had been made with the Russians that all German troops that reached American lines by midnight on 9 May would remain in American hands, and all German troops that entered after that time would be turned back to the Russians. Whether the Germans were aware of this agreement is unknown, but even without its ominous implications, German troops were rushing westward to escape the Russians in the tens of thousands.

Heavy Panzerspähwagens, most likely belonging to Stabskp./Pz.Aufkl.Abt.20 of 20.Panzer-Division, are surrendered to the US 16th Armoured Division in Pilsen, Czechoslovakia, 9 May 1945. Pz.Aufkl.Abt.20 had been ordered to move to Prague about 6 May after the German radio station in the city called for help: contact with the Abteilung was subsequently lost as communications deteriorated. At the head of the column is a Sd.Kfz.234/2 – the turret mounted smoke discharges are still loaded, and a German helmet and other gear cover the long fenders – followed by a motorcycle sidecar combination and a Sd.Kfz.234/3. Note the number of stowage lockers built into the fenders, and compare them to those on other Sd.Kfz.234s in this book.

NARA

Further along the column is another Sd.Kfz.234/2 and a unique Sd.Kfz.234 with 2cm Schwebelafette, seen here boxed in by civilian style cars. The Schwebelafette, usually seen on the Sd.Kfz.251/17, was a compact one-man turret with 360 degree traverse and full elevation that allowed heavier firepower than an MG to be brought to bear on ground and air targets at a moment's notice. The Sd.Kfz.234/2 demonstrates the vehicle's eight wheel steering arrangement, and shows this vehicle may have just pulled into line. **NARA**

In the back of the column, the leather clad crew of a Sd.Kfz.234/2 prep their vehicle in accordance with instructions from the Americans. One crewman pulls a toolbox from the stowage locker in the fender while another tends to turret details. The turret is cloaked in a camouflage net, leaving what appears to be a demarcation at the base of the turret, and it may be that the Americans have told the crewman to remove all camouflage from their vehicles before proceeding.
NARA

As the crewmen move about, tactical number '?24' can be seen neatly painted in front of the Balkenkreuz. Although they appear standard on the Sd.Kfz.234 series, it seems odd that the vehicles carry both the longer AFV jack as well as the short, round wheeled-vehicle jack seen above the muffler. The officer in the foreground is wearing a one-piece leather outfit, with zippers on the arms and legs. On his left breast, he wears a 1st class Iron Cross. **NARA**

A medic and other GI's check out progress on the lead Sd.Kfz.234/2 (identified by the helmet above the jerry can) as a crewman makes adjustments. The war is over, and everyone just wants to hurry up and be done with it. Note the open toolbox in the foreground and the horseshoe next to the driver's front visor. The thick rungs of the camouflage netting indicate that it may have been removed from a factory or some other stationary installation.

NARA

A rear 3/4 view of the lead Sd.Kfz.234 reveals that a large tarpaulin draped over the spare road wheel in the back has formed a rather large bustle. It's a hastily made arrangement and drags on the ground. The rear-facing driver's visors are opened up. Note the stowage box on the fender of the Sd.Kfz.234/3 in the foreground.   **NARA**

The column starts off, and the lead vehicle spews out a huge cloud of diesel fumes, obscuring the vehicles that follow. Unlike earlier German gasoline powered eight wheeled armoured cars, the Sd.Kfz.234 series had a Tatra 12-cylinder air-cooled diesel power plant. Although simpler and more fuel efficient, diesel engines do not burn fuel as completely as gasoline models, so expel more particulate matter and soot in their exhaust - all the more irritating to the crews' eyes and respiratory tracts.

3x NARA

GI's from the US 104th Infantry Division look over 'Rita', a Pz.Bef. Wg.IV Ausf.G or early H (note the plugged coaxial MG and tactical number starting '00'). The tank has a textbook Zimmerit coating and the remains of a whitewash paint job. **US Army via J.Nicholson**

A GI smugly smiles while posing with this Bergepanzer III; perhaps he knows just how rare photos of these vehicles will become in 60 years? The vehicle has become a tracked work of art courtesy of an 'ambush' camouflage scheme which has been sprayed using a stencil of some kind. The driver's KFF2 holes (above his armoured visor) have been plugged and the vehicle is missing the two large wooden beams usually carried either side of the superstructure. We do not know the unit or location, but the wheels and tracks are in excellent condition indicating minimal combat use.

L.Archer/W.Auerbach

While on the subject of the so-called 'ambush' camouflage scheme we have this colourful example of a Hummel photographed at an unknown location at an unknown date. This had been a late production example with boxed-in air inlets on the side of the superstructure and a full width driver's compartment - before someone rearranged it. A mysterious metal strap, now broken, was fastened around the gun, what was it for? **Ø.Leonsen, D.Campbell, D.Parker, C.Leeman**

A GI of the 75th Infantry Division peers into the hatch of a Hotchkiss H 39 in Ostheim, France, 31 January 1945. The little tank was known to the Wehrmacht as Pz.Kpfw.38 H 735(f) and has a cut down cupola; a standard German modification to give the commander better vision, but it lacks the distinctive aerial base at the rear of the fender. The trench spur is just visible on the rear. **US Army**

Cpl Otis Wideman of 1951st Ordnance Depot Co checks out a Pz.Kpfw.38(t) Ausf.C or D formerly of 4.Panzer-Division near Mannheim, Germany on 17 April 1945. The large circular hole in the driver's front plate was for the ball mounted MG 37(t) machine gun; the driver sat on the right. It retains the original Dunkelgrau paint. **US Army**

A GI poses on the turret of a Pz.Kpfw.IV Ausf.D with chassis number 80663 at a German training facility near Braunschweig, Germany. This vehicle has a Notek light first fitted to Ausf.Ds in February of 1940 but lacks the 30 mm armour that was added beginning in July 1940. The KFF2 driver's periscope appears plugged and a rudimentary angle iron rain guard is fitted over the driver's visor. It has the wider track and suspension components (introduced with the Ausf.F) and a tray for two spare road wheels on the left track guard (introduced with the Ausf.G). Most unusual is the neat addition of a 'C' hook to this tray, as Pz.Kpfw.IVs carried the more standard 'S' hook. Looking further aft, we see the brackets added to carry Triebgas cylinders, an alternative fuel to gasoline common to heavier AFVs relegated to driver trailing. A regulator fitted to the standard Maybach HL 120 TRM would have allowed the engine to burn this bottled gas.

L.Archer

This side view and the inset photos show that there were enough brackets to hold four Triebgas cylinders on the engine deck. Metal bands held them securely in place, and valves and tubing would have fed the four cylinders into one line before entering the engine compartment. The vehicle's jack is propped up by the idler. Note the rectangular engine air intake port and the degree to which the vision port projects from the turret hatch. The inside of the turret was a cramped, dangerous place to work. **L.Archer**

Men of the US 1st Army take a Pz.Kpfw.II for a joyride, probably at the same location as the tank on pages 30 and 31. This is no ordinary Pz.Kpfw.II, as it is the third Ausf.a/1 version off the production line, as denoted by the chassis number of 20003. Quite what it says underneath is a mystery. Both the 2cm Kw.K 30 and the MG34 have not been fitted as they are not required for driver training - see the 'Fahrschule' sign on the fender. **L.Archer**

A Panther Ausf.G photographed by George Gardin of C Company, 273rd Infantry Regiment, 69th Infantry Division around 4 May 1946. He had left Kassel by train for Le Havre and eventual return to the US. When the train stopped at Namur to pick up more GI's, he took this photo. He was told at the time that the tank was being shipped back to the USA for inspection and evaluation. It sports a battered coat of Zimmerit and hooks along the top of the turret for attaching spare tracks. Unfortunately we cannot identify its unit.   **G.Gardin**

A Canadian technical intelligence crew photographed this 4.7cm Pak (t) (Sfl.) auf Fgst.Pz.Kpfw.35 R 731(f) abandoned by the side of a road near Vught, just south of 's-Hertogenbosch in the Netherlands. It had been the property of 2./Pz.Jg.Abt.712 of 712.Infanterie-Division. The 4.7cm Pak (t) looks shorter than usual because the crew has rendered it unusable by draining the recoil cylinder before firing the last round.

LAC

Alkett converted 174 Pz.Kpfw.35.R 731(f) to 4.7cm Pak (t) (Sfl.) auf Fgst.Pz.Kpfw.35 R 731(f) between May and October 1941 and a further 26 were converted to command vehicles armed with a ball mounted MG34 instead of the 4.7cm Pak (t).

From this side view it could be that the Panzerjäger ran over a mine as the track is broken and the rear of the fender bent. The ammunition was kept in the 'bustle' at the rear of the superstructure with just 20mm of armour to keep it safe.   **LAC**

These two front views clearly show the details of the front armour and internal gun shield which, like other open topped Panzerjägers, moved 17.5 degrees to the left and the right with the gun. The hull of the Pz.Kpfw.35 R 731(f) was cast and it is interesting to see the shape of the armour above the driver's visor. With both crew doors open, we can see the location of the handles.   **LAC**

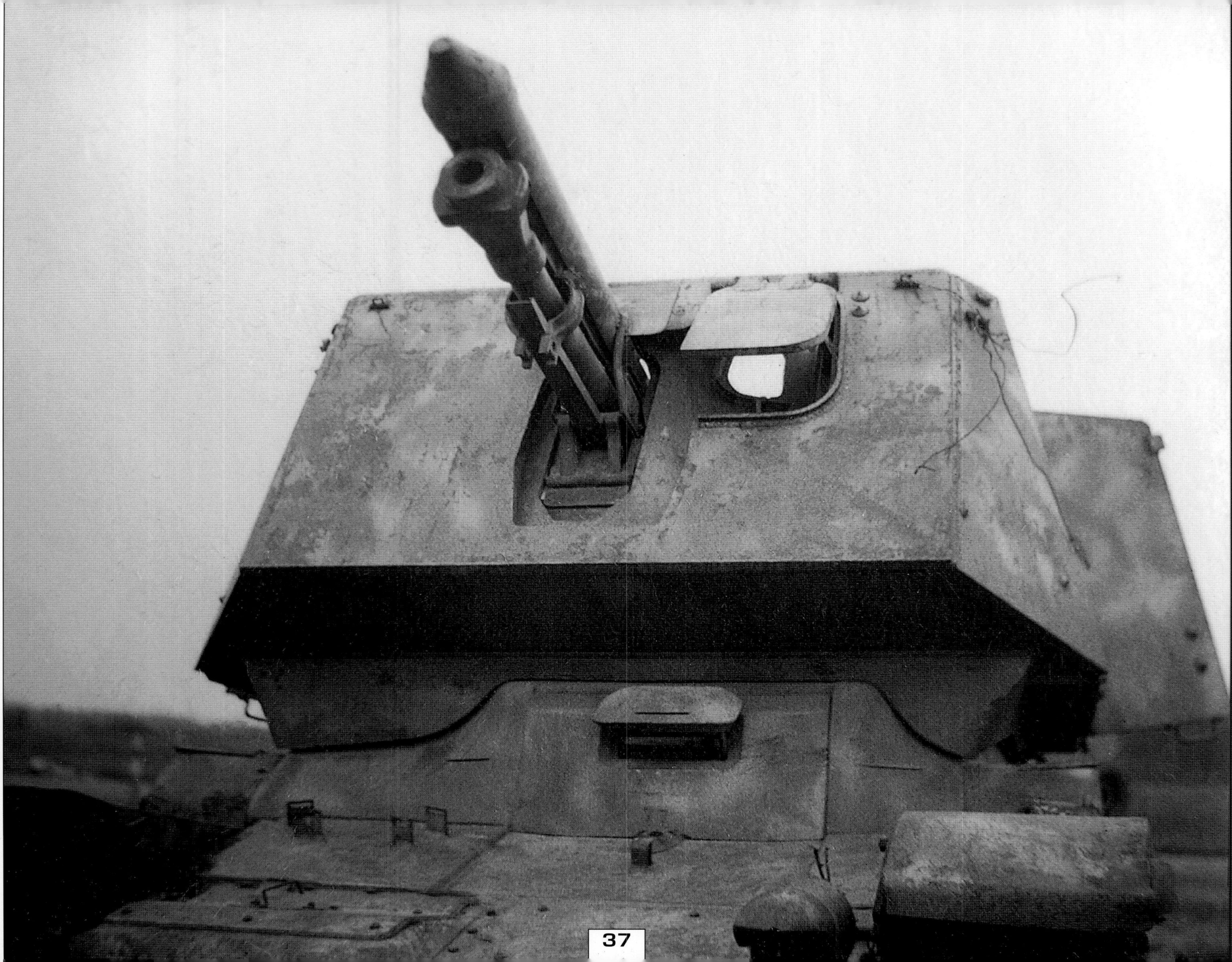

There is a triangular shaped vent underneath the 'bustle' of the superstructure but what is its purpose? Part of the engine deck is missing and the rear engine hatch opened, giving a partial view of the 5.8 litre Renault petrol engine, that could propel the little Panzerjäger to an exhilarating 20km/h. **LAC**

GI's from 97th Evacuation Hospital pose on the engine deck of an Ersatz M-10, one of 5 that had equipped I./Kampf.Abt.2150, Panzer Brigade 150 'Rabenhügel' during Operation Greif; the attempt to capture the Meuse bridges as if Americans. This example, coded B-10 had been the mount of Lt. Gerstenschlager, who was shot through the head. This highlights one of the deficiencies of the conversion; with the cupola removed, the commander had to stick his head out of the roof hatch - with fatal consequences. The tank was later taken over by Lt. Mandt (who previously had commanded tank B-4 before it struck a mine) and it was positioned near the cafe at La Falize, which is where this photograph was taken. We do not know who backed it into the café, or who pried open the chocolate vending machine.

C.Dijkhuizen

From the front, there is a passing resemblance to an M-10; the GI on the left has his boot in the opening left in the sheet metal cladding for the hull MG. The Germans had gone to some trouble to replicate some of the typically American details such as the lifting eyes on the glacis, the rounded front end, low towing points and footstep. The markings are for the 10th Armoured Regiment of the 5th Armoured Division.

C.Dijkhuizen

The Germans successfully disguised the shape of the hull and turret, but not those huge wheels. The tanks were painted in olive drab paint and markings applied by spray and stencil, you can see the overspray on the turret star. The turret disguise was achieved using sheet metal plates on an angle iron frame - part of this is visible at the top rear of the turret. A new US style gun travel lock fitted to the back of the engine deck replaced the one between the driver's and radio operator's hatches.

C.Dijkhuizen

41

A Pz.Kpfw.IV points skyward on the Wetstraat in Brussels early September 1944. Legend has it that it was knocked out by the resistance using a hand grenade, although self-destruction by the crew is more likely given the level of damage. The two most likely candidates for ownership are II./SS-Pz.Rgt.9 or 10.

2x L.Archer

About 3km south east of the Pz.Kpfw.IV on Boulevard Gen. Jacques is this old-timer in the shape of a Pz.Kpfw.17/18 R 730(f) or FT17. It is fitted with a Berliet turret mounting a 7.5mm Reibel machine gun. With a top speed of 8km/h, the two cyclists in the background will most likely overtake the little tank.
L.Archer

A pair of Sturmgeschütz III Ausf.Gs knocked out by US 9th Airforce fighter-bombers near Mödrath, Germany at the beginning of March 1945. One of them was in the process of being recovered, but which one? Note that the rear Sturmgeschütz is not fitted with the Rundumfeuer MG mount and does not appear to have the Pilze mounts on the superstructure roof, so clearly seen on the forward vehicle. Another view of the scene is on the front cover. **NARA**

Between 27 February and 3 March, 3.Panzergrenadier-Division defended the sector to the west of Mödrath, with 353.Infanterie-Division on its left flank and 12.Volksgrenadier-Division on its right. With the tactical number of '202' painted on the bow it would mean that these assault guns belonged to 2./ Pz.Abt.103 of 3.Panzergrenadier-Division. **NARA**

Most likely it was the lead vehicle that was being recovered as the starter crank cover and engine access hatches are open, that snake of tracks on the left being spare track carried on the rear. That tactical number also appears on the rear plate, quite unusually. Note the muzzle brake on the vehicle in the foreground is stuffed full of dirt. The close up on page 46 show the sprayed three-colour camouflage scheme to good effect.

2x NARA

A Sd.Kfz.251/3 Ausf.D Funkwagen, licence number WH 1738794, tows a Kubelwagen along the road as American trucks, moving in the opposite direction, carry fuel to stranded German units. This vehicle has the late war engine deck arrangement: the armour flap over the radiator has been left open to assist engine cooling.

NARA

The original film caption for the photos on pages 48 to 57 reads "GERMAN CONVOY NEAR KINZVART (?) Czech 9 May 1945: Convoy of German trucks, armoured cars, and other vehicles carrying surrendered German soldiers to assembly area." Kinsvart is the Hungarian name for Lazne Kynzvart, (German name Königswart), a spa town approximately 25km SE of Cheb. American vehicles appearing in the film, however, carry the bumper codes for the 803rd Tank Destroyer Battalion, organic to the US 5th Infantry Division, which attacked from Regen, Germany, towards Sušice, Czechoslovakia. In addition, several German softskins carry the emblem for FHH Pz. K, so it is believed that these vehicles belong to Stabskp./Korps-Pz.A.A. Feldherrnhalle and are actually in southern Czechoslovakia near Sušice or Vimperk instead of near Kinzvart. Also in Sušice in early May 45 was 1./Pz.A.A. 25, which had received 4 x Sd.Kfz.234/1 and 3 x Sd.Kfz.234/4 in mid March 1945.

Interesting details begin to emerge: the muffler sits especially high due to a shorter connecting pipe being used. Locks hang below the side stowage lockers. Two brackets, presumed to hold the Kurbelmast when not in use, are fixed to the vehicle sides. In addition to the Sternantenne and Kurbelmast, a third mount for another radio set is in the left rear corner. This vehicle was later filmed traveling through Netolice, Czechoslovakia, and the name 'Erika' could be seen chalked onto the engine side armour, barely visible here. **Inset:** Close up of the Kurbelmast, showing its mechanism for raising and lowering. **2x NARA**

"For want of a shoe, the horse was lost." This Sd.Kfz.234/4 Pakwagen is missing one of its front wheels, adding even more strain to an already overtaxed carriage. The gunner dangles his feet into the driver's compartment as if it were his favourite fishing hole while his loader relaxes opposite. The commander, standing in the fighting compartment, gives an idea of what his exposure would have been like in combat. One wonders if the vehicle could have been maneuvered into position quickly enough to hide its thin armour, or if the gun could have been sighted well enough to engage targets, while off kilter in this condition.

NARA

A close up of the vehicle from the side. The gun breech and muzzle brake are covered, but the gun barrel is not in its travel lock. Note that the centre rod for the bore cleaning brush is missing from its holder. Dust covers the factory-applied, hard edged camouflage paint scheme. An identical scheme is on the Pakwagen on page 54. The bracket in front of the commander is a Schwenkarm (swivelling arm) for an MG42.

NARA

More of the Pakwagen comes into view. Here we can see that the rear armour surrounding the fighting compartment is missing. The Pak 40 had a long recoil, and the armour may have been removed to give it more leeway. With sustained firing, the recuperator fluid would have gradually heated up and lost its effectiveness. A 'fire pause' mark would have let the gun crew know that its limits had been reached. What became of the rear facing driver's visor / position is unknown. Note that the rear fender stowage compartment does not appear to have a locking mechanism on it.
NARA

The vehicle is now in full view. Even entering into captivity, the Sd.Kfz.234/4 looks more like a greyhound set to run rather than a combat vehicle about to be retired. The light coloured 'Wehrmachtskanister' (jerry can) would have had a small, black disk on the handles to indicate it contained diesel fuel. The location of the few bits of foliage present leads us to believe the intent was to hide the large road wheels, a very distinct feature of the Sd.Kfz.234 series, rather than the vehicle itself.

NARA

The cameraman catches the column of vehicles as it recedes into the distance. Although of poor quality, one can make out a Sd.Kfz.234/1 at the tail end. Crew members, no longer concerned about Jabos, sit against the grenade screens of the 2cm Hangelafette turret. A Sd.Kfz.234/1 was usually paired with a Sd.Kfz.234/3 support vehicle to form a 'Panzerspähtrupp,' the smallest element in a recon platoon, but the latter was superceded by the Sd.Kfz.234/4 starting in December of 1944 as the war situation became critical. The lines in the photo are downed telephone lines.
NARA

A blurry photo of another Sd.Kfz.234/4 in the same column depicts the nonchalance of peace. The crew lounges on the vehicle under sunny skies: a week earlier, and the skies would have been full of artillery shells, rockets and bombs. This vehicle carries an extra passenger, since the normal crew was four. The rods for the bore cleaning brush are missing.

NARA

A camouflaged leichte Schützenpanzerwagen Sd.Kfz.250 'neu' Funkwagen moves along in convoy towards captivity. Unfortunately, branches hide any unit emblems, tactical signs or numbers. A late V3000 follows.
NARA

Armoured car - literally. A Kriegsmarine unit has armoured their m.E.Pkw. Typ 40 around the crew compartment and the radiator and given it a fresh camouflage scheme. Following up is a Mercedes-Benz L1500A in a darker colour, probably Dunkelgrau. **Top**: From left to right; a late Ford V3000, an earlier example with colourful camouflage and a Mercedes-Benz L3000 with a Holzvergasser.   **NARA**

Top: Women, children and German soldiers ride into American lines in May 1945. The Zundapp KS 750 motorcycle and Kubelwagen carry the emblem for IV Pz. Korps. **Bottom:** Soldiers turn to a Steyr 1500A/02 l.gl.Lkw and Adler 3 Gd Pkw for transportation.

4x NARA

Another Sd.Kfz.250 'neu' Funkwagen passes in front of the camera. Because of the towrope draped along its left side, this vehicle could be identified as passing through Netolice, Czechoslovakia, later on.

NARA

Here's an anachronism, a Krupp L 2 H 143 Kfz.69 in near pristine condition carrying the tactical sign for an armoured Panzergrenadier company. **NARA**

This Sd.Kfz.251/3 carries the lucky leaf (Klee) emblem of IV.Pz.Korps in honour of its CO, Gen.d.Pz.Trp Ulrich Kleemann. The Korps was later renamed Feldherrnhalle, but some members of Panzerkorps-Nachrichten-Abteilung 44 saw fit to retain the old unit emblem.
NARA

Sd.Kfz.251/3 Ausf.D Funkwagens of FHH Pz.K. on the move. The original caption for this film segment covering pages 58-65 reads "Surrender: Sušice, Czechoslovakia 9 May 1945… long column of German troops in trucks, halftracks, ambulances, and motorcycles moves along highway near Winterberg, Czech, under US MP escort." Winterberg is also known as Vimperk. The US 5th Infantry Division occupied Vimperk until 21 May 45. The vehicle on this page carries licence plate number WH 1738793. **NARA**

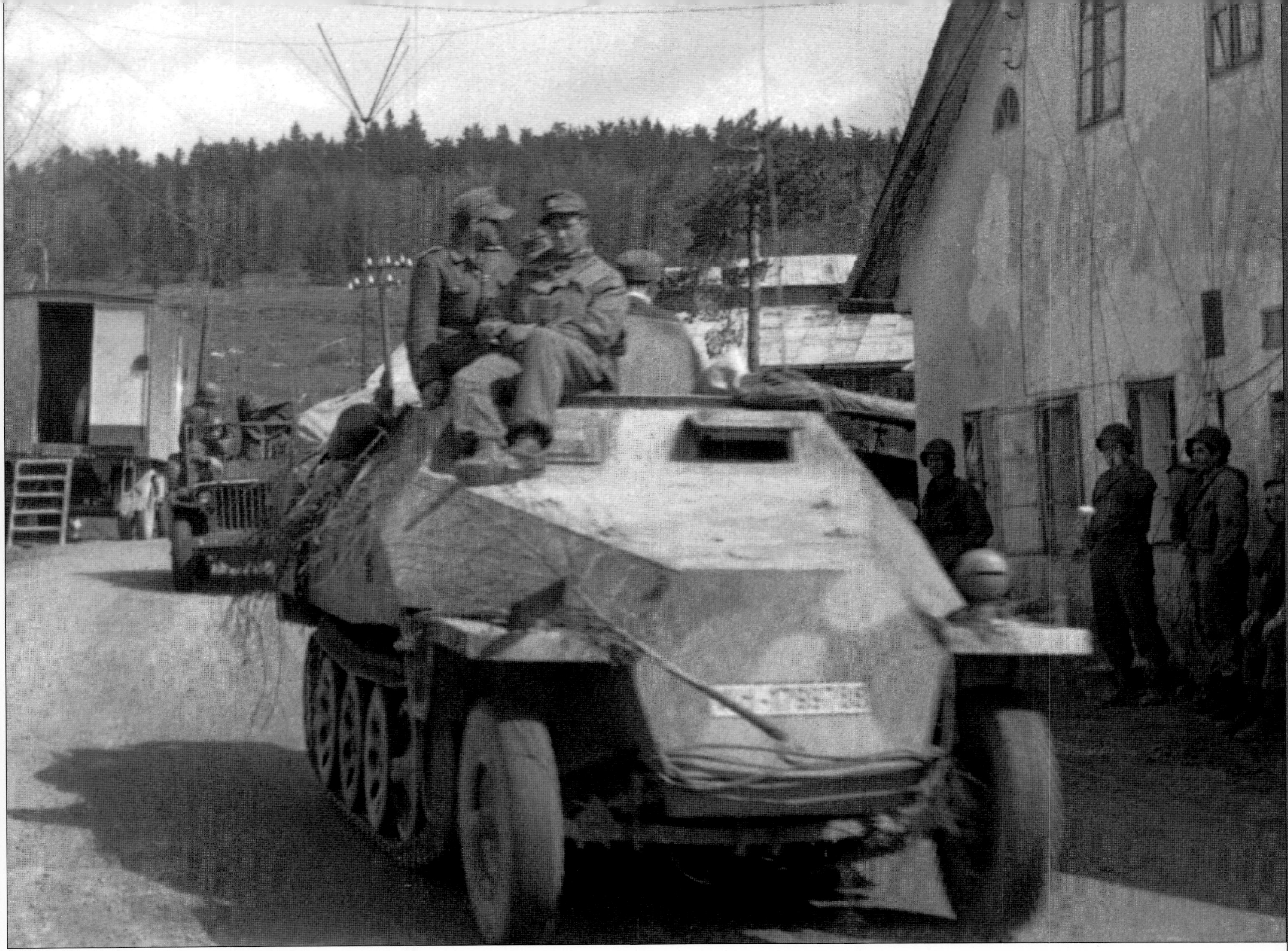

Another Sd.Kfz.251/3 with late war engine deck.
The crewman in the rear sits atop the radio racks.
Brackets of some sort have been fitted between
the front visors, reason unknown.   **NARA**

At the end of the column is a Kfz.13 armoured car on its last reconnaissance. First manufactured in 1933 as a cheap means of providing a scout car for the Wehrmacht, this one appears to be in relatively good condition, right down to the Balkenkreuz on its windshield. Where it came from we do not know, but no matter: the war is over, and the roads would soon be clogged with displaced persons, camp inmates, prisoners of war and others seeking medical attention, refuge and food. **NARA**

The road to Büllingen after the failure of 12.SS Panzer-Division to capture Domaine Bütgenbach. The picture was taken on 1 February 1945. From the left we have a Pz.Beob.Wg.IV or Pz.Bef.Wg.IV Ausf.J of 12.SS Panzer-Division still with its Sternantenne fitted to the rear and vehicle antenna on the turret roof. Behind this is Jagdpanther 134 from s.Pz.Jg.Abt.560 whose barrel has been truncated (probably by US forces) and behind this is a Pz.Kpfw.IV that has been pushed onto its side. On the other side of the road is a Pz.IV/70(V) of SS-Pz.Jg.Abt.12.

US Army

66

Smoking kills. A Pz.Bef.Wg.IV Ausf.J burns on 13 April 1945 for W.J. Tomko, a US Signal Corps film cameraman with the 166th Signal Photo Battalion, attached to the US 6th Armoured Division. Given the unit and the date, the tank was probably near Zeitz, South of Leipzig. The only Panzer unit in this area was 11.Panzer-Division, although their tactical numbers were normally painted in black, not the white we see here. The tank has Flammentöter exhausts and four return rollers. **NARA**

78.Sturm-Division lost this Pz.Kpfw.38(t) Ausf.C or D in the Olomouc – Boskovice area of Czechoslovakia in late March or early April 1945. Something has smashed away the 15mm armour on the turret and hull side, creating a large crack down the hull side into the bargain. The vehicle takes on quite a different look without the 775mm diameter roadwheels, their leaf springs now being visible. The round object in the foreground looks to be a Romanian helmet.

M.Solar

Stripped naked would be the best description for this Sturmgeschütz III Ausf.G pushed into a ditch near Rochefort, Belgium sometime after the failure of Wacht am Rhein. It had been a 2.Panzer-Division vehicle, belonging to either II./Pz.Rgt.3, St./Pz.Jg.Abt.38 or 2./Pz.Jg.Abt.38 while part of Kampfgruppe Holtmeyer. It was pushed off the road into a ditch and The protruding edges painted white to improve visibility and prevent accidents.

L.Archer

A Bulgarian soldier checks out the engine vents on a RSO/01 in the Cakovec area of Croatia in April 1945. The divisional sign on the front is that of 16.SS-Panzergrandier-Division. It has a sprayed camouflage pattern over the Dunkelgelb basecoat.

MPAB

The Bulgarian 1st Guards Division captured this RSO/01 in Niska Banja, east of Nis, Serbia on 11 October 1944. It has a faded whitewash paint finish and, unusually for a German vehicle, a camouflage net over the tilt which has been fixed to the windscreen wipers. The loading stencil on the cab door is different in both photos. **MPAB**

A lovely comparison of how fixtures and fittings, even gun barrels, disappear from a Panzer wreck. The II./Pz.Rgt.15, 11.Panzer-Division lost this Pz.Kpfw.IV after a run in with the US 90th Infantry Division near Všeruby, Czechoslovakia. It appears to have an Ausf.G hull and late Ausf.J turret - note the swiveling commander's hatch.

The tank must have been used without the front elements of the turret Schürzen as the tactical number '15' has been painted directly onto the turret. The wreck was frequently visited (and plundered) by people from the local villages.

2x J.Podhorský via M.Solar

Bulgarian soldiers check out a Pz.Kpfw M42 738(i) in Nis, Serbia around 15 October 1944. It had been used by Pz.Abt.z.b.V.12. The tank had carried a reasonable amount of spare track, some of which has fallen to the ground, to give a little extra security but the little tank was still woefully lacking in protection. The drive sprocket has four retainers fixed to the outside to prevent the track from climbing off. This was a modification introduced by the Germans during 1944. The amoeba camouflage scheme, also introduced in 1944, was applied at the factory and consisted of red brown and green edged with sand yellow.

2x MPAB

Two louvred grilles are missing from the engine deck exposing part of the FIAT-SPA V-8 petrol engine. The object on the other side of the engine deck is an external fuel tank and the curved object on the turret roof is the mount for the AA MG.

The shoeless boy is leaning against what is left of the 4.7cm gun, which the crew probably sabotaged.

MPAB

A Panther Ausf.D photographed by Ralph Durenburger of the 275th Infantry Regiment, US 70th Infantry Division in Germany 1945. The location is given as "on the side of the road from Rothenburg an der Fulda to Bebra." Given the location, it would have belonged to Pz.Lehr-Abt. Bergen or Pz.Ausb.Abt.1, both of these units being subordinated to Pz.Ausb.Verband Franken.

S.Dixon

These photographs were captioned as being taken in Scheren by a GI of the 8th Infantry Division. If we assume that he meant Schwerin, the Sd.Kfz.234/1 would have belonged to Pz.Aufkl.Abt.125, 25.Panzergrenadier-Division, who surrendered to the 8th at Schwerin during March of 1945. It is a later production example with two stowage lockers along the side. A pair of headphones replaces the gunsight to the left of the 2cm Kw.K.38.

2x W.Auerbach

During 1938, M.A.N. produced four prototype 8x8 medium weight trucks, which were subsequently reworked as amphibians. Until now nothing has been known about their fate - well here is one photographed by a GI at the end of the War. This is one of two fitted with a 40-ton winch, spade (seen at the rear) and plough for road demolition and removal of obstructions. Behind the cab were two 150bhp M.A.N. V8 diesel engines, which drove the roadwheels or propellers and included a power take-off for the winch. The two large round plates at the front covered the headlamps, the two smaller ones were covers for tow cables from a secondary winch. Note the inset steps and turn signal on the side of the vehicle.

W.Auerbach

We pictured this Marder 38T in Panzerwrecks 1 while at a collection point in Utrecht, this is it with other AFVs on 10 May 1945 at Armsfoot. The crew has written the name 'Sofi' on its bow and drawn a bird by the driver's visor. The crew has not long departed as a pair of headphones is hanging over the fighting compartment. To the left: a Bergepanzer III, complete with a ZF SSG 77 Aphon transmission (for Pz.Kpfw.III or Sturmgeschütz III) on top. It lacks the wooden superstructure of the example on page 26 and carries a full set of Schürzen, but the large oblong plugs for the driver's periscopes are the same. One of the poles for the Behelfskran has been left on the fender and is just visible under the chin of the Canadian officer.

LAC

The photographer takes a few steps to the right and captures, in addition to the Marder, an old Sturmgeschütz III Ausf.C/D and a pair of late Ausf.Gs. The late Gs are excellent examples with Rundumfeuer MG mount, coaxial MG and an impressive tally of kills (18 and 16). Each also has two names on its nose. The Ausf.C/D has a unit insignia on the mudguard and three kill rings on the barrel - including one for an aircraft - and has been retrofitted with an armoured shield for the loader's MG. The names Elsa, Nelly, Mitzi and Erika have been written in Fraktur on the noses of the vehicles.

LAC

Still at the Armsfoot depot. The Ford V3000 on the left is a Maultier (the track can just be seen behind the wheel of the Kettenkrad), it belongs to the I-Staffel of an unidentified unit and has been fitted with an Einheits cab. In the background, the two Flak vehicles are interesting. The Ford V3000 on the left may be a Maultier or a truck "it is difficult to tell", but the top of the cab has been removed to allow better target tracking for the 2cm Flak 38. The Sd.Kfz.10/5 next to it has an interrupter fitted behind the cab to inhibit the depression of the gun and so prevent the crew from shooting up their vehicle. Both guns have kill rings around their barrels. **LAC**

GI's attach a tow chain to an immobilized Sd.Kfz.7/2 flakwagen. The inevitable detritus of war, including mines, booby traps and unexploded ordnance, had to be cleared off roads to continue the advance.

US Army

OVERLEAF

The turret of a Sd.Kfz.123 Luchs sits atop a Sd.Kfz.234 chassis somewhere at war's end, location, date and unit unknown. The blotches on the glacis are dusty boot prints, not part of the camouflage scheme. Martin Block attempts an explanation: "The Kriegsgliederung of 17.PD dated 1.3.1945 listed '2 Pz.Sp.W.Luchs' with Stabskp./ Pz.A.A.17, although no deliveries of any type of recce car were recorded for the division in 1945. On 8.3.45, the division reported having '2 Pz.Sp.Wg.Luchs II.' The Kriegsgliederung dated 1.4.45 listed '1 Pz.Sp.W.Luchs,' this time in 1.Pz. A.A.17." Is this the hybrid we see here? If so, where did the chassis come from? Mr. Block continues: "In mid March 1945, Pz.A.A.'Sternberg,' part of Pz.Brig.103, was incorporated into Pz.A.A.17. This latter unit, Pz.A.A.'Sternberg,' had in turn been formed from 1./Pz.A.A.190 of 90.Pz. Gren.Div in late January 1945, and had received 12 s.Pz.Späh-Wg during Dec 44 - Jan 45. Maybe the Pz.Werkst.Kp. decided to turn two damaged vehicles into one operational? In the final weeks of the war, 17 Pz.Div. crossed from Troppau to Tabor. Elements of 17 Pz.Div. made it to American lines at Pisek but were handed over to the Russians just a few days later."

2x NARA

A dug in Panther Ausf.G destroyed by the 6th Russian Guards Tank Army behind the barracks in Vyškov, Czechoslovakia in late April 1945. The most likely German unit was I./Pz.Rgt.27, 19.Panzer-Division who fought in this area from 27 April. The turret has been liberally clad with spare tracks and has a painted tactical number of 215. It is interesting that the Schürzen have a completely different camouflage pattern to that of the tank.

J.Holíček via M.Solar

From the sublime to the ridiculous. This old Pz.Kpfw.I Ausf.A lost a track and was abandoned on Pratecky Hill, near Brno, Czechoslovakia. At this point in the war, the slow, lightly armoured tank armed with a pair of machine guns would have been of little value, other than for training. It lacks an exhaust muffler (missing from the fender) so it would have made quite an entrance too. The crew has obliterated the Balkenkreuz on the hull side, possibly with mud. **V.Kos via M.Solar**

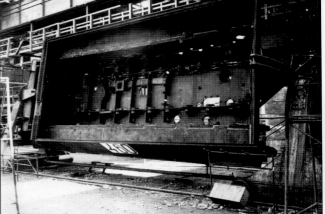
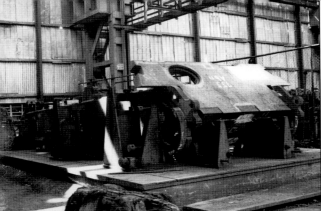

The following series of images was shot by a USAF cameraman by the name of Pryer at the end of the war, his mission: to film some of the major industrial targets of the US Airforce. Here he captured the Henschel & Sohn plant in Kassel-Mittelfeld where they assembled the Tiger II tanks. The basic armour hull was fabricated primarily by Krupp, as seen in the top three photos (which were not shot by Pryer), then shipped to Henschel for finishing and assembly. On arrival at Henschel, the holes in the hull sides were machined for the suspension components. This can been seen above, where the holes appear shiny in comparison to those on the hulls in the background.

5x NARA

Wegmann, also in Kassel, assembled the turrets for the Tiger II. Here we see some of the final production turrets that would have been fitted had the US Army not overrun the plant in March 1945. They have three notable changes: the addition of five loops on each side for holding camouflage material, six sets of spare track hangers on each side of the turret for the new single track links (for the new 18 tooth drive sprockets), and a small post on the commander's cupola for the swiveling AA MG mount (in lieu of the ring over the periscopes). Note the Tiger I turret in the foreground of this page.

2x NARA

When you examine the turrets you start to see subtle differences; the turret in the centre of the photo has two marks on the turret side - armour plugs perhaps? The second and third turrets from the right on page 93 have no fittings welded to their sides, although they have weld marks. These turrets also have no commander's cupolas. In the background, a loader's hatch sticks up - of pre July 1944 vintage, old stock we presume. These turrets were mounted on dollies that ran on rails.

2x NARA

92

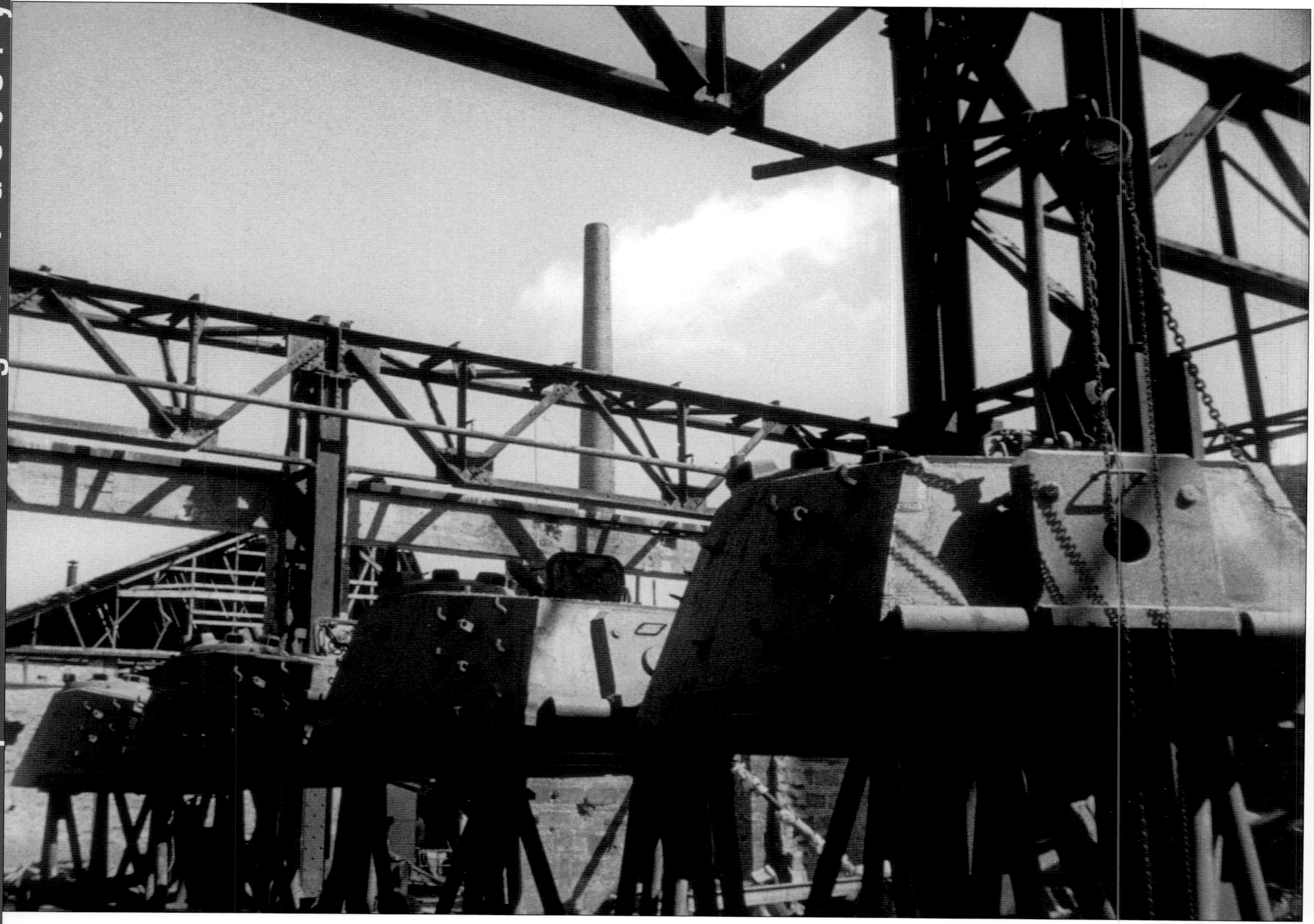

Page 94: At some point during production, the rear turret hatch was simplified. It differs in having two circular protrusions, presumably for the simplified latches.
Page 95: Among the debris, a pair of Maybach HL 230 P30 engines each capable of moving the 70,000kg Tiger II at up to 38km/h. The sheet metal objects stacked on the right are trackguards that would be bolted to the hull sides.   **2x NARA**

Standard production turrets elsewhere in the factory grounds sitting on a different pattern of dolly. It is interesting to note that the turret in the foreground has spare track hangers on its sides, but not the lugs underneath. These are present on the turrets in the background.

Ø.Leonsen, D.Campbell, D.Parker, C.Leeman